AF489296

WRITTEN AND ILLUSTRATED BY JONNO H

ISBN 9798884699465

WWW.LAWNDARTBOOKS.COM

THE ARTWORK FOR THIS BOOK
WAS CREATED DIGITALLY.

FIRST EDITION

YOU MADE A POO!

So you sat down on the loo,
It looks as though
you've made a poo.
Just for fun, let's name it **Stu**.

When you flush, what will your poo do?
5

Around the toilet bowl Stu's spinning,
But his journey is just beginning!

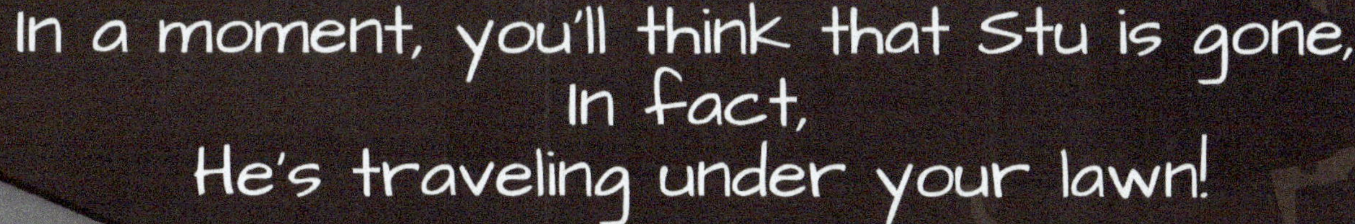

In a moment, you'll think that Stu is gone,
In fact,
He's traveling under your lawn!

Stu tumbles about and splashes around,
making new friends from all over town.

There are Poos
made of food from France and Ukraine,
China, Korea, Slovakia and Spain.

So much variety to be found in the drain!

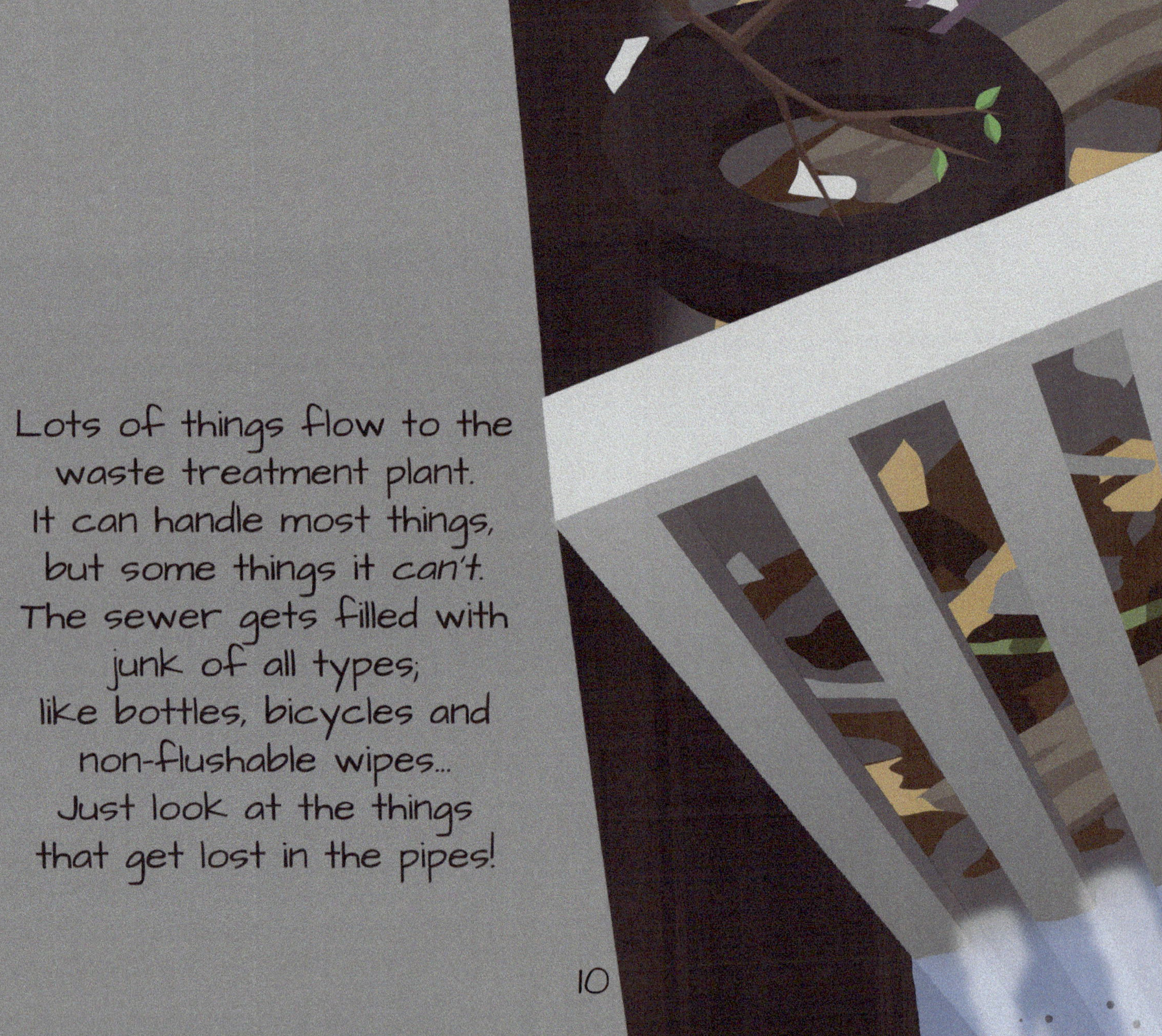

Lots of things flow to the
waste treatment plant.
It can handle most things,
but some things it can't.
The sewer gets filled with
junk of all types;
like bottles, bicycles and
non-flushable wipes...
Just look at the things
that get lost in the pipes!

Screens like this let
the proper things
through,
like water and paper
and poos like Stu.
They're meant to
filter the things we
don't flush
like garbage or
branches or an old
plastic brush.

HELLO! WELCOME TO THE
SETTLING TANK
NO DIVING

Stu enters a tank designed to remove grit.
To do this the water is slowed down just a bit.
Gravity pulls sand and little rocks down,
until only the floaty light stuff moves around.

Into an aeration tank,
we pump in warm air,
to encourage the
microbes and germs
living there.

Stu will be sitting for a hour or two. So, let's pause to take a **closer look** at your poo.

When your body needs to get rid of dead cells, they go out with your poo.
Some parts of food don't break down, like leafy fibers or corn. They're easy to see.
Most importantly, there are lots of germs, called "fecal bacteria" in your poo.

You might think Stu is made of food.
But inside's stuff you never chewed.
Toxins and fats
seeds, husks and bile.
Old cells your body
throws out after a while.

The most important thing Stu has inside
are the **bacteria** coming along for the ride.

Fecal bacteria, like the one you see here
help you break down your poo.
They hang out in your gut,
and escape out your butt
Living in, and chewing on, Stu.

What bacteria does is great for you,
but not so much for our friend Stu.
As around the aeration tank Stu is lazing,
the bacteria and germs are grazing.

A gas called methane he's emitting.
Into tiny parts he's splitting.
To say the least, Stu is worse for wear.
But there is no need to despair.

(He's just a poo, he does not care.)

20

Before long, there's not much left of Stu.
Just nitrogen, sulfur and CO2.

A gas called methane adds to the mix,
along with Stu's undigestible bits.

The **clarifier tank** is their very next stop,
where some stuff will sink and some rise
to the top.

The bacteria sink with the
rest of the muck,
which for them leads to some
incredible luck.

Because while the rest of Stu
floats away,
the germy **sludge** gets used in
other ways.

A lot of germs are still
along for the ride,
And we don't want them getting to the
water outside.
So the water is directed
to a tank where it's disinfected.

Ultraviolet light comes from sunlight
too much will give you a burn.
For the germs that made it this far,
it becomes their main concern.

Using light to fry the germs
may seem a little *mean*,
but it's the only way to be sure
the water is completely clean.

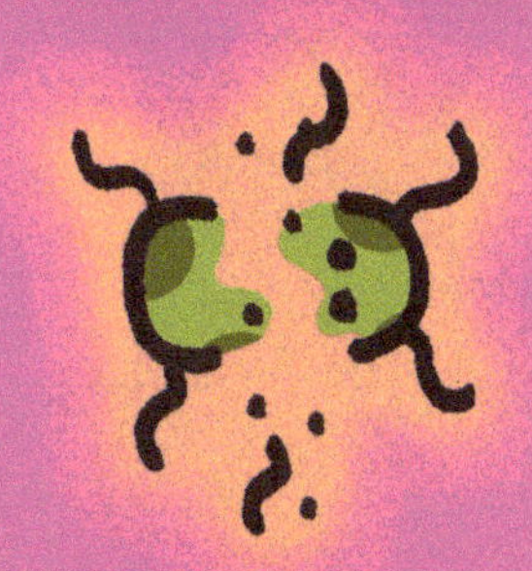

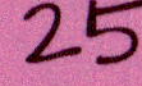

Now that the water is sparkly-clean,
it's released into a nearby stream.
The little bits that once were Stu,
will soon feed plants that will soon feed you!

Soon, you'll use the 'loo,
and discover when you're through,
that you've made another poo.

Now you know what it will do!